ats

ST. MARY SCHOOL
LIBRARY

Title IV

WORLD OF RACING

STOCK CARS

By Sylvia Wilkinson

Consultants:
 Wayne Hartman
 John Morton
 Roman A. Kuzma

CHILDRENS PRESS, CHICAGO

Richard Petty's Monte Carlo

PICTURE ACKNOWLEDGMENTS:

Jan Bigelow—pages 2, 4, 8, 9 (2), 10, 11, 12 (2), 15, 16, 17, 20, 23 (2), 25 (2), 26, 27 (2), 28, 31, 32 (3), 33, 34, 35, 37, 38, 39, 40, 41 (2), 42

Rocky Moran—pages 5, 6, 18, 36

Dan Mahoney—pages 7, 13, 21, 22

Len Meents—page 14

Library of Congress Cataloging in Publication Data
Wilkinson, Sylvia, 1940-
  Stock cars.

  (World of racing)
  SUMMARY: Describes stock car racing and the cars that perform in this solely American sport.
    1. Automobile racing—United States—Juvenile literature.   2. Petty, Richard—Juvenile literature.   3. Moran, Rocky—Juvenile literature.   [1. Automobile racing.   2. Automobiles, Racing]   I. Bigelow, Jan.   II. Title.   III. Series.
GV1033.W54   796.7'2'0973   80-27729
ISBN 0-516-04715-9

Copyright© 1981 by Regensteiner Publishing Enterprises, Inc. All rights reserved. Published simultaneously in Canada. Printed in the United States of America.

4 5 6 7 8 9 10 R 90 89 88 87 86 85 84 83 82

INTRODUCTION

"Lee Petty was the smartest race driver I ever saw. When I raced Daddy, he beat me like a dang drum."

Those are the words of "King Richard" Petty, the winningest stock car driver of all time. Now Richard has reached the age that matches the number on his famous race car—43—and he too is the father of a stock car racer, Kyle Petty. And he too can beat his son "like a dang drum."

Race after race, the same drivers win in stock car racing. But unlike most champion athletes, they are not all young. The most famous NASCAR* drivers: Richard Petty, Bobby Allison, Cale Yarborough, and David Pearson, are middle-aged. The 1980 "Rookie of the Year," Jody Ridley, is 38 years old.

Stock car racing is solely American racing. American automobiles, such as Plymouth and Chevrolet, made in car factories in Detroit, are raced with American drivers at the wheel. Most of their races are at tracks in the South. Stock car drivers race constantly; a normal season has 36 races.

So you see how stock car drivers "get smart." Experience is the best teacher.

*NASCAR: National Association for Stock Car Auto Racing

DRIVING A STOCK CAR

But even Richard Petty was once a *rookie*. Let's talk to two drivers. One is Richard Petty, a champion whose racing wins have made him a millionaire. The other is stock car rookie, Rocky Moran, a go-kart winner from Pasedena, California, who decided to try his hand driving the big cars.

Chris Economaki, the well-known race announcer, is famous for asking drivers: "What's it like out there?"

Good question. When we sit in the stands, watching the powerful cars roar past, our heartbeats quicken. We can smell hot rubber and burning fuel. But we are only spectators, not behind the wheel of a charging machine, our throttle to the floor.

Sportscaster interviews a driver before a race at Pocono International Raceway in Pennsylvania. Pocono is a paved oval track.

Rocky Moran poses beside his Chevrolet sponsored by the Daisy Shoppe.

Let's ask stock car rookie, Rocky Moran, the question: "What's it like out there, Rocky?"

Rocky replies: "Incredible! It's really hot shut up in there. It's so hot the floor burns your feet. On an oval track, there are cars floating around outside at 175 miles per hour."

Rocky Moran racing his F.K.E. 2 Kart

Rocky learned how to race cars as a road racer in sports cars. He raced on the twisty courses at Watkins Glen and Road Atlanta, in lightweight, quick-steering road racing cars. Also, though it is hard to imagine, this 240-pound driver was once F.K.E.* 2 Kart National Champion, racing around the track in a vehicle lighter than he is. It seems much more natural for Rocky to put his defensive-lineman-size body into a two-ton stock car. This is the heaviest, strongest car racing anywhere in the world.

*F.K.E.: Formula Kart Experimental

Rocky Moran drives a Buick at Ontario Motor Speedway.

Then Rocky got his chance to race on the two-and-a-half-mile oval in Ontario, California, in a stock car. He said, "The first thing that knocks you over about driving a stock car is you brake with your *left* foot."

Think about driving a normal "stick shift" car. There are three pedals: on the left is the clutch, on the right is the brake and the gas. When racing a stock car, you use your left foot on the brake so you'll have your right foot free to give it gas at the same time.

"I started out using the brake all wrong. I was driving the stock car like a sports car. In a sports car, you go deep into each turn then stand on the brakes. I did this at first in the stock car. In practice, my laptimes were way off the other guys. The car felt out of balance. I talked to veteran driver, Jimmy Insolo. He said in a stock car you brake from the time you turn off the wall to the apex (middle) of the turn. Squeeze the pedal down like pulling the trigger of a gun, not a sudden jerky motion. You keep giving it gas with your right foot even though you're braking. I tried it and right away, it felt better and I went faster."

Drivers Chuck Bown and Dave Marcis on the track at Pocono

Ronnie Thomas (right) and other drivers (below) line up for the start of a race at Pocono.

On the fast, high-banked oval tracks, the cars reach 175 to 180 mph on the "straights" and slow only to 140 through the turns. No shifting is used to slow the car, only the brakes and the turning motion.

"I had started out treating a Grand National* car like a sports car," Rocky explains. "It didn't take me long to realize it wasn't going to act like one. I had to adjust, not the car. Before a driver starts asking the crew to make changes on the car, he has to figure out how much of the problem is him."

*Grand National: late model stock car

Jody Ridley, NASCAR Rookie of the Year in 1980

The race car felt strange to Rocky from the first time he sat behind the wheel. "I was used to a little steering wheel that was very responsive to turning. Think about a clock. You hold your hands at 10 o'clock and 2 o'clock in a sports car. A tiny twitch of the wheel in a sports car makes it jump. Also, in a sports car, you're in a reclining position.

"When you drive a stock car, you sit straight up. The car has a big steering wheel. You have to turn the wheel to 12 o'clock and 6 o'clock to get enough steering action to throw it into the turn. You have to really work the wheel because it has such slow reaction."

Rocky found the most important adjustment wasn't inside the car. It was outside. "The traffic runs so close together, *every lap* is like the start of a Can-Am race," Rocky tells us. "Cars are all around you out there going 175 miles per hour. The cars are so heavy and strong, those guys don't think twice about brushing the wall, getting a 'Darlington stripe.'"

Bobby Wawak, Baxter Price, and Roger Hamby jockey for position.

Lake Speed's car bears a scar far worse than a Darlington stripe.

A Darlington stripe is the mark on a race car from touching the wall. It is named after a South Carolina track that has probably put "stripes" on every stock car driver's car. As you can imagine, some of these "Darlington stripes" can qualify as dents!

Rocky says, "Turbulence off other cars becomes a big factor. You have to understand *drafting* to understand what is happening in a stock car race."

Rick Newson's Oldsmobile, after backing into the wall, is being hauled away for extensive repairs.

Drafting

A common sight in a race on the big oval is two stock cars running nose to tail at 180 miles per hour. They are drafting. In a draft the engine doesn't run any faster, but the car moves through the wind better. If two cars are able to run at 180 mph alone, by drafting each other, they can race at 183 mph.

What causes this increase in speed?

Cale Yarborough (#11), Dale Earnhart (#2), and Darrell Waltrip (#88) draft at Ontario Motor Speedway in California.

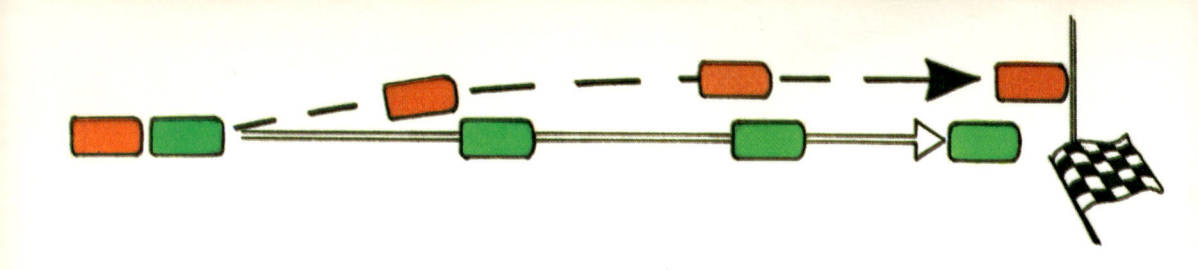

When two cars are *drafting,* the front car punches a hole in the air. Imagine this: a fish swimming in the water creates a space where there is no water, the space the fish is occupying. In the same way a moving car creates a space where the air has been pushed aside. Although we can't see the air or the absence of air, a race car can feel it and respond to it.

Air causes *resistance* to a moving object. A car must use up some of its power to push the air out of its way. The air that has been shoved aside will come back together. But if the *second* car can run very close to the rear of the *first* car, it can take advantage of the dead space. The second car doesn't have to shove the air out of the way because the first car has already done it. The second car can travel faster this way than it can travel alone.

Also, a slower car can run with a faster car because the slower car doesn't have to use up its power shoving the air aside. It's a little like going through a crowd of people, following a big guy and letting him clear the way.

Another interesting fact is that two cars can travel faster than one. This gives the first car an advantage too, the 3-mph increase that we spoke of earlier. Why? Because two cars together form a more streamlined, aerodynamic shape than one car alone. This accounts for the 3-mile-per-hour increase for *both* cars. It also explains why the first car doesn't try to shake the tag-along behind him.

Car #67 moves out preparing to slingshot pass the lead car #52

To fall out of a draft or "lose the draft" can be costly to a stock car racer. Drivers participating in the "buddy system" of drafting will soon leave a lone car behind.

Highly-skilled drivers can run 180 mph and actually *touch* the other car. Richard Petty says, "A lot of drivers get spooked by running wheel-to-wheel at 180 mph and beating on each other. As far as hitting the other car, you can do it just as good at 180 mph as at 100 because there's only a mile or two per hour difference between the two cars. As long as you don't hit something that's sitting still, you're all right."

Richard Petty (#43) runs wheel-to-wheel with Buddy Baker.

Stock cars enter races in tip-top shape, but they often leave the track like this car did at Pocono.

Rocky, who admits that drafting "spooked" him at first, found out: "When someone drafts you, your car gets loose. The air they're pushing makes your car's tail move out. The suck from a draft is so powerful, you start running with guys who are faster than you. Once Parnelli Jones took advantage of my inexperience. I was running seventh and had passed him. He started drafting me and I got loose. Then he hit my bumper and I lost it and hit the wall. It cost me five positions."

Petty says, "I've hit guys before, guys I've lapped (passed) a bunch of times who didn't belong out there racing. You can bend fenders in stock car racing without killing one another."

Rocky Moran's accident in his first stock car race at Ontario. (Rocky's car is nearest the wall.)

Every race driver remembers his first race. Rocky recalls, "I had the worst accident of my career in my first race. A guy in front of me got sucked into a draft and he lost it. When he spun, I went into his door. Another car hit him, then five more. When something happens, the cars literally disappear into their own tire smoke. You don't know where you are, but if you lose it, you go to the wall. You can't go off in the dirt to miss it all. I broke my leg and a bunch of ribs in that one."

Richard Petty left for his first race with words from his father who was racing somewhere else the same night: "Richard, if you expect to make it in anything, you have to try a little bit harder than the rest. I don't care if you're a clown in a circus or trying to sell pots and pans, you have to work harder than the next man if you want to be the best." Richard proved that was good advice.

Richard describes that first race: "I qualified thirteenth, right in the middle of the pack. I remember sitting in the car real calm. Then the race started and cars was passing me right and left and dirt was flying through the air. I blew my cool.

Richard Petty and Buddy Baker in one of Pocono's banked turns

"I drove that car every which way but straight. I never did spin out, but I bounced off the wall a bunch of times. We had big ol' bumpers on the car and I tore the right rear bumper right off it.

"The big deal I remember about that race, we were coming off the number-four corner down the straightaway and Joe Weatherly blew a tire and went right through the grandstand fence. There were boards and things flying everywhere and I put my hands up over my face. It was just an automatic thing, and when I realized I'd taken my hands off the steering wheel I couldn't believe it and it like to have scared me to death. I said, 'Man, I can't be doing this!' But I just kept on doin' it."

Rocky Moran brings his Buick out of a turn at Ontario.

So how do you learn to race? Sounds as if you jump in and give it a go. Rocky tells us, "The good drivers will give you advice, basic stuff on setting up your car and the gears. The main thing they tell you is to run low on the track. In other words, get down there out of their way."

Richard Petty says no one can tell you how to drive. You have to discover the best way for you. Richard, who is known for running high on the track, found that was where he felt "natural," the first time he raced. Also he followed the faster drivers around the track. He kept up with them as best he could in his rookie year, trying to imitate their driving techniques.

Rocky Moran (#58) being overtaken by Richard Petty (#43) at Riverside International Raceway

Then, twenty years later, with Petty as the master driver, Rocky Moran used the same approach. "At Riverside in a NASCAR road race, Petty, Pearson, and Yarborough came up behind me to lap me. That really got me psyched. For two laps, about five miles, I hooked up with them. That was the high point of the race for me, seeing how those guys drove the race track. In the esses (a series of turns shaped like the letter S) I picked up three-quarters of a second just from seeing how the fast guys did it, and following them. When they radioed me my times, I was amazed. I was going fast enough to have qualified twenty positions higher than I did. Then they got away from me and my bubble broke. But it was great while it lasted.

Cale Yarborough

"When you drive lightweight, fragile sports cars, you drive with a different attitude towards the machinery. Well, pip, pip, we turn here," he jokes in a British accent. "Those stock car guys go tearing through the esses, and if there's asphalt under the car, O.K., dirt, that's O.K. too. Who cares!"

Petty, who admits to difficulty on road courses, sums up the difference—oval racing is between cars; road racing is between you and the road. Richard Petty claims if you start paying too much attention to the other cars in a road race and forget about the road, a turn will come up and you'll run off the track.

Richard Petty

"That's not to say the stock car guys aren't smooth drivers," Rocky adds. "They're really smooth on the high-speed ovals, never upsetting the tire adhesion. They can drive as if their cars are on a string. If you have a strong, heavy machine you have a different attitude towards its endurance.

"Also, the regular drivers have tremendous physical endurance. I wear myself out partly because I don't have their feel. That only comes with experience. Stock car drivers never seem to get hurt like the good Formula One drivers, for example. They live long enough and have long enough careers to have marketable names. But stock cars are safer. There is no comparison to the danger you confront in a Formula One or Indy car. Stock cars are bigger and heavier, and there's a lot more around you to protect you."

There're a thousand little tricks to be learned in stock car racing. For example, Richard Petty has all his gauges tilted so that when the engine is operating properly, all of the needles will point up. This means a quick glance is enough to size up the condition of his motor. He looks in his mirror twice each lap, once on each "straight." This routine means he can keep his eyes almost constantly on his competition.

Benny Parsons (right) signs autographs for his fans wearing his boots. Tim Richmond (below) with his helmet on, adjusts his seat belts before the start of a race.

Instead of wearing thin leather driving shoes, like a sports car racer, Petty wears boots. Because the engine is in the front and the exhaust pipe passes under the floor, a driver's feet get so hot that blisters will form on them in a long race. The heat is so intense inside the closed cars that drivers sweat off as much as ten pounds during a race. Petty wears a special "cool hat" inside his helmet to keep his body temperature down.

Rocky notes, "You even have to pad your seat differently in a stock car. All the turns go to the left so you pad the right." Creature comfort is important if a driver is to remain alert for an entire race.

25

Trucks haul a stock car, extra wheels, and spare parts to race tracks throughout the United States.

On the short tracks that range from one-fifth mile to the more popular half-mile oval, a driver may complete the circle every 20 seconds, 500 times in a row. Asked if it made him dizzy, Richard Petty answered no. But he added it was easy to get "dislocated" and forget which turn you are in. That is dangerous since there is a special "groove" or path the driver takes through each individual turn.

How popular is stock car racing in the United States? In the South, where it originated, it is the number one sport. There are tracks outside the South now where stock cars run: Riverside and Ontario, California; Pocono, Pennsylvania, and Michigan International to name four. Many of the drivers reach hero status. For example, Richard Petty has the largest fan club of any professional athlete.

Look at the Pocono stands on Friday (above) and then on race day (below). On his pace lap at Riverside, Rocky Moran was amazed at the attendance: "I never look in the stands when I road race, but I was suddenly aware that I had never seen so many people at a race before."

Neil Bonnett and Cale Yarborough positioned in starting line up at Pocono.

Because of the close competition and because the caution flag system erases a driver's lead each time there is an incident on the track, there is never a dull moment in stock car racing. The end of practically every race is a down-to-the-wire thriller. As Richard Petty says:

"Most race drivers are very impatient. They won't wait for things to happen, they've got to make them happen. Nine out of ten do their racing at the beginning of the race, but I do mine at the end. In a 500-mile race, you run the first 490 miles for exercise."

HISTORY OF STOCK CARS

The automobile was designed to be transportation, to carry people from Point A to Point B. Before the fuel crisis, designers concentrated on comfort and speed, not economy of fuel. In this country and overseas, from the first moment an automobile was run, men have tried to build a *faster* automobile, to travel the fastest from Point A to Point B. Part of the car's purpose was to get there; another was to get there first. In other words, from the beginning, to *race* cars seemed the natural thing to do.

One of the early uses of fast cars in this country was *illegal*. To avoid government taxes and licenses for making alcoholic beverages, "moonshiners" made liquor with illegal "stills" (an apparatus used to turn corn into alcohol). Drivers carried this liquor by moonlight in fast, "hopped-up" cars, 1940 Fords with Cadillac engines, racing from the stills to the distributors. Two of these drivers, Curtis Turner and Junior Johnson, became living legends. Both were former bootleggers who became stock car racing heroes.

Two forms of American racing—drag racing (the fastest time in a quarter mile) and stock car racing—began illegally on public roads. Then these activities became sports competitions. Their popularity grew rapidly because of the American fascination with speed and the automobile.

In the late '30s, drivers made long runs on Daytona Beach. A race was held there in 1936 with cars running in a circle for the first time. All the competitors got stuck in the sand, but the idea caught on. After prison terms were handed down, moonshining lost much of its financial attraction. Drivers decided to make their livings on the legal race track doing the same thing—building and driving fast cars.

After World War II when more people could afford cars, the interest in racing grew. In 1948 a driver named Bill France organized NASCAR, the National Association for Stock Car Auto Racing, which still exists today. In 1949 the first *new* car race was held in Charlotte, North Carolina. Many of the cars that competed are no longer manufactured: Henry J's, Hudsons, Nashes, Studebakers, Packards. The first winner was a Lincoln.

Racing stock cars is big business. Companies are eager to support a winning driver and advertise their products (right).

Map of the 2.5 mile superspeedway at Daytona (below). Because of the kink at the start/finish line this shape is called a tri-oval.

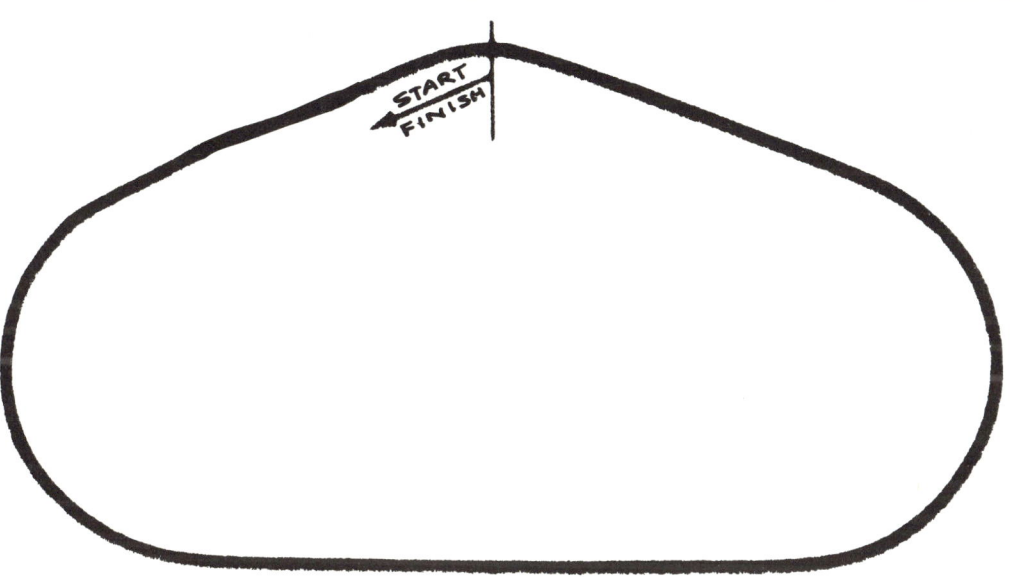

In 1950 the famous "superspeedway" at Darlington was built by a man named Harold Brasington who owned some earth-moving equipment and went to see the Indy 500 and got inspired. Not long after, Bill France built a speedway at Daytona Beach, paved and high-banked, leaving the sand for the tourists. The Detroit car factories got involved because winning races was the best advertisement money could buy.

31

In order to keep the competition fair, cars must meet certain standards. Here we see official inspectors using templates to check for illegal body modifications. Each stock car must conform with the rules and have the safety features required by NASCAR before it can compete.

Today's stock car drivers are good businessmen as well as good drivers. Their cars are no longer "stock" cars either. The Fords, Plymouths, and Chevrolets you see on the stock car tracks have been built for racing "from the ground up" by racing teams instead of factory assembly lines. As Richard Petty says, "My race car gets built from scratch."

There are two major concerns in the construction of a stock car: speed and safety. Let's examine the safety features that make stock cars the world's safest cars.

After the chassis is completed, the fabricators build the *roll cage*. It is literally a cage—a strong steel tube structure to house the driver and to make the car rigid. It protects the driver in crashes and roll overs.

Doors on a stock car do not open, so the driver enters through the window opening. To completely cage himself after he is inside, the driver hooks a net in this window. This net keeps his head, shoulder, and arm inside during a roll over or if he hits a wall on the driver's side.

Close-up of the net in position

Because of the removal of the inner fender panels, the mechanic (on the right) can stand inside during an engine change.

After the roll cage is complete, the car is built around it, with body panels and suspension attached to the proper points. In the past, cars were "chopped down" from "stock" or factory constructed cars. The inside was stripped, taking out the comfort features such as padding, upholstery, and radios. A special racing seat was welded in the bare interior. Now "stock" cars are built "from scratch." They are still called "stock" but they are as far from stock as a car can get.

Using a hoist, mechanics lift an engine.

The end result is a lighter, stronger racer. This race car is frequently given a fresh motor. The motors are restricted to 358 cubic inches, so teams are constantly working to find more than the 500-plus horsepower they are now getting.

Since the death of Fireball Roberts from burns, fuel cells have been used. A fuel cell is a container consisting of a rubber bladder filled with special foam. Unlike a formula or Can-Am car where the driver is surrounded by fuel, the stock car cell is in the trunk, a long way from the driver, and only holds 22 gallons. For comparison, a Formula One car holds up to 66 gallons. In addition, for fire safety the cars have fire extinguishers, and their fuel pumps stop when the engine stops running.

Stock cars are the least "aerodynamic" race cars. Their large, blocky shape can only be streamlined so much. The "hole" they must make in the air is far larger than, say, a Super Vee, which is only about 25 miles an hour slower than a stock car. Because of their aerodynamic weakness, stock cars depend on *power* and *handling*.

Like all stock cars, Rocky Moran's Chevy has a large frontal area.

Crew refuels and changes tires on Buddy Baker's stock car.

On the long ovals such as Ontario and the superspeedways at Talladega and Daytona, although handling is a factor, *power* is the most important element. The cars are "flat out," full speed ahead, for long stretches. On the short tracks on the Grand National circuit such as Martinsville, North Wilkesboro, and Bristol, and on the road courses, *handling* is the key feature.

If a car is not handling properly, a quick remedy is to change the *wedge*. This can even be done during a race. The driver can radio his instructions to the crew and, while they are fueling and changing tires, a crew member can adjust the wedge. This is achieved by screwing one rear wheel lower than the other.

Baxter Price's pit crew works frantically to get his car ready to re-enter the race at Pocono.

To demonstrate changing the wedge, take a chair. Each leg represents a wheel. Put a stack of pennies under the left rear leg or "wheel." This is the equivalent of "adding weight" or lowering the wheel. What happens to the left front leg? It leaves the ground or "gets lighter" while the right front leg is pressed harder to the ground. Changing the length of a chair leg always causes the same thing to happen on the *opposite* corner. A car works the same way: add weight to the left rear and you add weight to the right front.

Crew member checks tire pressure.

Two other terms you will hear are *push* (understeer) and *loose* (oversteer). A *pushing* car is one that wants to go straight when you try to turn it. A *loose* car is one that tends to break away, or lose adhesion, in the rear. Stock car drivers use the terms push and loose; sports car drivers say understeer and oversteer. They mean the same thing. Jokingly, a pushing car wants to hit the wall with the front end; a loose car wants to hit it with the rear. A neutral car hits it with both ends at the same time.

The driver reports the handling conditions to the crew. The handling can be affected by an oily surface, the banking or angle of the road, wind, etc., as well as the car itself. The crew makes adjustments that will make the car *neutral*, which is the absence of understeer or oversteer. Actually, neutral isn't necessarily the perfect setup. A stock car is more stable to drive with a slight push; in other words, the absence of looseness in the back and the presence of a tendency to go straight.

To further complicate matters, for qualifying, the car is set up differently, with a tendency towards *loose*. Because each driver has the whole track to himself, he can have a loose car with the tail hanging out and not have to worry about hitting other cars. He only runs two laps this way to determine his starting position. His racing laps will be more conservative and his car will be returned to the slight *push* state.

For a short race, teams use fifteen or more tires. For a 500-miler, more than 20. Most tires are changed on the right side on the ovals because outside tires wear out faster. Impact wrenches are used to remove the five lug nuts on each wheel. These wrenches must be driven by nitrogen to prevent sparks which create a fire danger. The wheels are heavy, over 90 pounds, and after running hard, tire temperature is over 200 degrees. To avoid fumbling nuts during a fast tire change, crew men have even held fresh nuts in their mouths. Now most of them glue a set in place on each fresh wheel.

In a single race, drivers can go through 15 to 20 or more tires, depending upon the length of the race.

Right: A long stick is used to clean the windshield of Neil Bonnett's stock car during a pit stop.

Below: STP crew talks to Richard Petty.

Did you think the driver had a few seconds to rest during a pit stop? Coming in at about 100 miles an hour on a super-speedway, the driver has to stop the car exactly in his pit, a space about the size of a parking place. Overshooting can cost him a race. He puts the car in low gear and holds on the brakes so the wheels won't turn while his tires are changed. He keeps the motor revved up. Gas is put in with 11-gallon cans, over 80 pounds for the crewman to lift over his head.

Only five men can service the car, so a long stick is used to clean the windshield, brush out the radiator screens, and give the driver a cup of water. He has to swallow quickly because in 15 seconds, his crew will have the fuel in and the tires changed. Hardly the same as having a "time out!"

Checkered flag at Pocono

And when a driver sees the checkered flag at the end of the race, he knows the work must now *begin*—preparation for next weekend!

Glossary

aerodynamics: the branch of dynamics that deals with the force of air on a moving object such as a race car. Stock cars are the least "aerodynamic" of modern race cars because of their large frontal area and box-like shape.

apex: the point in a corner where the car comes closest to the inside of the road, where corner entry ends and exit begins

back marker: a car/driver running near the back of the pack, in the last rows of the grid

back off: let off the throttle, slow down

balance: the state of a car's handling characteristics as related to "loose" (oversteer) and "push" (understeer). The best balance for most drivers is neutral to a little understeer. (see loose and push)

bank (banking, high banked): degree of inclination or angle of the road in a turn, characteristic of superspeedway (see oval)

blown engine: an engine that has failed, usually with many broken parts. Examples: He *blew* his motor when he overrevved. The *blown* engine had a hole in the block. (Blown engine also means supercharged engine, one using a *blower* to force air into the cylinder)

bore: the diameter of a cylinder (see cylinder)

camber: A car wheel is perpendicular to the road. Camber is the degree it is moved from this perpendicular state, for example negative camber means the wheel goes out at the bottom, positive camber means it goes in at the bottom.

Can-Am: a North American *(Can*adian-*Am*erican) racing series for envelope bodied, 1631 + lb., open cockpit, high powered cars that are built for racing only and are raced on closed (road racing) circuits

carburetor: an apparatus on an internal combustion engine that mixes fuel with air, sending it into the combustion chamber in vapor form by suction from the piston. Stock cars use a single four-barrel carburetor. (A barrel is a passage for the fuel/air mixture into the intake manifold)

caution flag: see flags

chute: straight part of the track (see straight)

cool hat, cool suit: a special garment worn under a driver's fireproof clothing that has tubes that circulate cool water on a driver's head or body, fed by a small reservoir mounted in the car

cylinder: a chamber in an internal combustion engine through which a piston moves driven by the combustion process. Stock cars use 8 cylinder, American engines.

Darlington stripe: a scrape down the right side of a stock car caused by brushing the wall, named after the superspeedway

drafting (slipstreaming, getting a tow): following a car closely, letting the lead car punch a hole in the air, taking advantage of the decreased wind resistance. Also the lead car has the advantage of being part of a more aerodynamic shape formed by two or more cars.

drag racing: a type of racing that involves two cars, running a timed one-quarter mile straight. The loser is "eliminated" and another challenger takes on the winner.

dump can: an 11 gallon fuel container that is manually lifted by one crew member during refueling.

headers: the part of the exhaust system that attaches to the cylinder heads to carry off burned gases from the engine, a performance improvement which replaces the more restrictive exhaust manifold

impact wrench: a heavy duty, nitrogen-driven wrench used on race car wheel nuts

Indy (Champ, Championship) car: a high powered, single seat, open cockpit and open-wheel car used in North American competition, primarily oval track such as Indianapolis and Pocono, some road racing

lap: (1) noun - a complete circuit of a race course (2) verb - If Driver #1 is so far ahead, he has completed one more *lap* than Driver #2, #1 is *lapping* #2 at the moment he passes him. If #2 manages to get back in front of #1, he has put himself back on the same lap as #1, or he has *unlapped* himself. This means that a caution flag (see flags) situation could put #2 close behind #1, because all of the cars on the same *lap* are bunched up again for a restart.

loose (oversteer): tendency of a car to steer into a turn more than intended with the rear end losing adhesion and swinging to the outside (see push for opposite)

esses: on a road course, a continuous series of left and right turns shaped like the letter "S"

flags: a signal system, displayed in turns and at the start/finish line.
    caution flag: yellow flag displayed when there is danger on the track, cars slow and do not pass, the pace car returns to the track for a restart that takes place when the danger has been removed. The caution flag is very important in stock car racing because it erases any lead that cars on the same lap have, giving the fans constant "new" races to watch when the track is green (start and restart flag) again.
    white flag: in oval racing (stock, Champ and sprint), it means one lap to go. In road racing it means an emergency vehicle is on the circuit.
    red flag: stop the race, extreme danger
    black flag: go to the pits on the next lap
    blue with yellow diagonal stripe: a faster car is behind you; get out of his way.
    black and white checkered: end of race

flat out: full throttle

formula: a set of rules or specifications for a race car, usually open-wheel, single seat, and open cockpit

fuel cell: the fire-safety container to hold fuel in a race car that consists of a metal or plastic structure with a rubber bladder filled with sponge-like material. A stock car has a 22 gallon fuel cell in the trunk.

Formula One (Grand Prix, GP, F1) car: a high powered, advance design, single seat, open cockpit, open-wheel race car used in the most important international road racing competition, winner is called World Champion

groove: the fastest route around an oval. Road racers use a different word—*line.* There is one difference between the two words: track conditions can cause the *groove* to change, while *line* seldom varies.

go-kart: the smallest racing vehicle made, consisting of a seat, frame, four tiny wheels, a motor (usually 100 cc. 2 stroke Yamaha), and simple brake, clutch and chain-driven axle. Go-karts are often driven in competition by young people, too young to race (or drive) automobiles

Grand National: an event and a type of car in a NASCAR series for late model American stock cars (no more than two years old)

handling: the car's reaction to the manual controls, i.e., braking, accelerating, steering. Examples: The large sedan *handled* like a sports car. Wide tires improved the car's *handling*.

lose it: lose control of a car

manifold: a chamber that (1) takes the fuel-air mixture from the carburetor to the cylinder head (intake manifold) or (2) takes the exhaust from the cylinders to the exhaust pipes (exhaust manifold)

mount: to assemble a tire and wheel. Example: He *mounted* a fresh set of tires on the rear wheels.

NASCAR: National Association of Stock Car Auto Racing, the major ruling body for stock car racing

oval: an oval shaped race track. There are several types of ovals: (1) short tracks - 1/8 to 5/8 mile, dirt or paved, such as Myrtle Beach (dirt) or Martinsville (paved) (2) long tracks - 1 mile to 2.6 miles, used also for Indy cars, such as Pocono or Ontario (3) superspeedways-high banked, long ovals, such as Daytona, Darlington, or Talledega

pace car: a car used to lead the competitors in a race through pace (or warmup) laps and/or to lead the competitors for a restart after a caution flag (see flags), but does not participate in the race, pulling off the track before the green flag waves

pace lap: a lap taken by the competitors before the start of a race to warm up the cars and to prepare for a moving start. This is sometimes mistakenly called a parade lap. A parade lap is a much slower lap preceding the pace lap (or laps) to allow the spectators to see the cars.

pit, pits, working pits, pitted: The pit area is beside the track, usually on a straightaway, and is used for refueling and servicing of the cars. Examples: He drove into the *pits* with a blown tire. He *pitted* the car. He made a *pit* stop under the yellow flag. He was assigned *pit* #5. He charged down the *pit* lane (road).

push (understeer): tendency of a car to steer less sharply than intended, with the front end tending to go straight (see loose for opposite)

qualifying: an on-track session where a driver demonstrates his speed in relation to other car/driver combinations, determining his starting position and/or whether he can reach the speed required to run the race. Examples: There are three *qualifying* sessions. He failed to *qualify*. *Qualifying* begins at noon. His *qualifying* time places him in the third row. Note: Stock cars qualify one at a time while Can-Am cars qualify all at once.

racing slick: a wide, flat surface (treadless) tire used for racing only. Stock car slicks have an "inner liner" for safety which inflates when the tire blows so the driver can make it to the pits.

radiator: a nest of tubes with a large surface area exposed to moving air to cool its circulating fluid contents: water or oil (also called oil cooler)

redline: the maximum safe rotation speed of an engine, usually indicated by a red line on the tachometer dial. Some tachs have an additional indicator called a "telltale" (tattletale) that sticks at the highest revs the driver turns, tattling to the mechanics if he overrevs the engine. Stock car engines redline at around 7,500 rpm's.

revolutions (revs, rpm's): revolutions per minute of an engine. Also used as a verb: Petty *revved* up his engine.

road racing: a form of racing that takes place on closed circuits designed to resemble a country road with a variety of turns and hills, such as Riverside.

roll cage: structure made of steel tubes used primarily in sedans (enclosed or "closed" cars) to protect the driver in a turnover by keeping the roof from caving in. Roll *bars* are generally used in open cars.

rookie: a driver in his first season of racing. An experienced driver is called a veteran. A veteran can become a rookie again if he tries a different form of racing. For example, Richard Petty would be called a rookie if he tried to qualify for the Indy 500.

short track: see oval

shut the door (gate): to block another driver by moving in front of him on the groove (or line) through a turn

slingshotting: a technique for passing requiring a drafting situation where the car that is behind uses the reserve momentum he has gained by drafting to shoot out of the slipstream and go around the lead car (see drafting)

small block Chevy: a production engine manufactured by Chevrolet from 305 cubic inches (used in Can-Am cars) to 350 (used in stock cars). The large block Chevy is the 396, 427, and 454. The modified small block is the most widely used racing engine in history. Stock cars are restricted to 358 cu. ins.

spin: to go out of control and revolve. A driver can "spin out" and stay on course, or "spin off" the track.

spoiler: an air deflector used on the front and rear of many GT cars or sedans to give downforce by redirecting airflow over and under the car.

sports car: small, usually two seat and open (convertible) car used for transportation on public roads, known for cornering ability and driving pleasure, also a car of the above description set up for racing.

stick, bite: In racing terms, *stick* means adhesion in general. Example: The tires are *sticking* well. *Bite* means traction coming off a turn. Example: The rear wheels were getting more *bite*.

stick shift: a manual transmission that requires the driver to move a gearshift lever (stick) to change gear ratios, used in reference to street cars (see transmission)

stock car: an unmodified car, just as it came off the assembly line. That is the dictionary definition, but a stock car used in NASCAR racing by drivers like Richard Petty is a highly modified car. So if you mean "unmodified," say: "the car is stock;" if you mean what Petty drives, say "stock car."

straight (straightaway): the part of a race track that travels in a straight line, therefore the fastest part of the track

stroke: (1) distance the piston travels in the cylinder (noun) (2) to drive slowly, conserving the car (verb)

superspeedway: see oval

Super Vee: a small, approx. 950 lb., open-wheel, single seat, rear engined racer (formula car) using a 180 horsepower VW Rabbit engine and many VW parts

suspension: the system of springs, shocks and linkages that suspend the main structure of the car from the wheels. The suspension cushions the shock from an uneven road surface. It keeps the wheels in contact with the road so the front wheels can steer and the rear wheels can use the engine power efficiently.

tachometer (tach): a gauge on the dashboard that indicates how fast the engine is rotating, for example the safe top rotation speed for a 358 cu. in. small block Chevy in a stock car is approx. 7,500 rpm's (see redline)

T-bone: to strike a car broadside (or in the door) with the front of another car, forming a "T" shape

V: engine design such as V6 or V8 where cylinders are arranged in two rows that form a "V"

transmission (gearbox): the portion of the drive train that transfers the engine revolutions (power) to wheel revolutions (drive). The transmission allows the driver to select the proper gear ratio for the speed of the car. Gears come in sets of two, a big gear and a little gear. The relation of the number of teeth is the ratio. A stock car has four forward gears and a reverse. On ovals, the transmission is only used when starting from a stop. On road racing courses, stock car drivers must shift gears for turns.

wedge: a term referring to a chassis adjustment that changes the weight distribution on all four wheels to gain a desirable handling characteristic. Visualize putting a wedge under the leg of a chair. The weight distribution of all four legs changes.

window net: a strong net hooked into the window opening on the driver's side after he is inside to keep his head, left shoulder, and arm inside should the car roll over.

Index

accidents, 19, 20
aerodynamics, 36
air resistance, 14
Allison, Bobby, 3
boots, driving, 25
braking, stock car, 7
Brasington, Harold, 31
Bristol race course, 37
buddy system, 16
building a stock car, 32-34
Can-Am race cars, 35
Can-Am races, 11
caution flag system, 28
changing the wedge, 37, 38
Charlotte, North Carolina, 30
checkered flag, 41
Chevrolet cars, 3, 32
construction of a stock car, 32-34
Darlington, South Carolina, race course, 12, 31
Darlington stripe, 11, 12
Daytona Beach, Florida, race course, 30, 31, 37
"dislocation," 26
doors, stock car, 33
draft, losing the, 16
drafting, 12-17
drag racing, 30
Economaki, Chris, 4

esses (turns), 22
fire safety, 35
first race, driver's, 19, 20
F.K.E., 6
Ford cars, 29, 32
Formula Kart Experimental, 6
Formula One drivers, 24
Formula One race cars, 35
France, Bill, 30, 31
fuel cells, 35
gauges, tilted, 24
go-karts, 4
Grand National circuit, 37
Grand National stock car, 9
grooves, turning, 26
handling, stock car, 36-39
heat, inside race car, 25
Henry J cars, 30
history of stock cars, 29-31
Hudson cars, 30
illegal racing, 30
illegal use of fast cars, 29
Indy car, 24
Indy 500 race, 31
Insolo, Jimmy, 8
Johnson, Junior, 29
Jones, Parnelli, 17
karts, 4, 6
learning to race, 21

Lincoln cars, 30
liquor, illegal driving of, 29
loose (oversteer), 39, 40
losing the draft, 16
Martinsville race course, 37
Michigan International race course, 26
moonshining, 29, 30
Moran, Rocky, 4-12, 17, 19, 21, 22, 24, 25, 27
motors, stock car, 35
NASCAR, 3, 22, 30
Nash cars, 30
National Association for Stock Car Auto Racing, 3, 22, 30
neutral car, 39
North Wilkesboro race course, 37
Ontario, California, race course, 7, 26, 37
oval racing, 23
oversteer (loose), 39, 40
Packard cars, 30
Pasadena, California, 4
Pearson, David, 3, 22
Petty, Kyle, 3
Petty, Lee, 3, 19
Petty, Richard, 3, 4, 16, 17, 19-26, 28, 32
physical endurance, 24
pit stops, 41

Plymouth cars, 3, 32
Pocono, Pennsylvania, race course, 26, 27
popularity, stock car racing, 26, 27
power, stock car, 36, 37
push (understeer), 39, 40
Riverside, California, race course, 22, 26, 27
Road Atlanta race course, 6
road racing, 23
Roberts, Fireball, 35
roll cage, 33, 34
rookies, 4, 5, 21
safety features, 33-35
season, stock car racing, 3
seat pads, 25
servicing, pit stop, 41
shoes, driving, 25
speed increase, drafting, 13-15
speeds, stock car racing, 9
steering wheel, stock car, 10
stripe, Darlington, 11, 12
Studebaker cars, 30
Super Vee race cars, 36
Talladega race course, 3
tires, 40, 41
turbulence, 12
Turner, Curtis, 29
understeer (push), 39, 4
Watkins Glen race cour
Weatherly, Joe, 20
wedge, changing the, 3
wheels, 40, 41
windows, stock cars, 33
Yarborough, Cale, 3, 22

About the Author

Sylvia Wilkinson was born in Durham, North Carolina and studied at the University of North Caro Hollins College, and Stanford University. She has taught at UNC, William and Mary, Sweet Briar Col and held numerous writer-in-residence posts. Her awards include a Eugene Saxton Memorial Trust G A Wallace Stegner Creative Writing Fellowship, a *Mademoiselle* Merit Award for Literature, two Sir W Raleigh Awards for Literature, a National Endowment for the Arts Grant, and a Guggenheim Fellow In addition to four novels, she has written a nonfiction work on auto racing: *The Stainless Steel Carro* adventure series on auto racing; an education handbook; and articles for *Sports Illustrated, Mademoi Ingenue, True, The American Scholar, The Writer,* and others. Her four novels: *Moss on the North Side, A K Frost, Cale,* and *Shadow of the Mountain* are available in Pocket editions. A fifth novel, *Bone of My Bones* just been sold to G.P. Putnam's.

Sylvia Wilkinson is head timer and scorer for Paul Newman's Can-Am racing team. She also timed 1980 Daytona 24 hour and Le Mans.